Contents

Introduction 3
The "why" and the "how" 4
Step 1: The Plan 7
Step 2: Who should produce the content? 10
Step 3: What kind of content to produce? 11
Step 4: How to produce and distribute your content? 14
Step 5: How to get an audience for your content? 17
Step 6: How to transform your readers into clients? 20
Step 7: Monitor your content and the results it brings you. 23
Golden rules of content marketing 25
A few words in the end 32

©2015 Important note: This document is protected by copyright laws and contains material proprietary to Maria Ruxandra Burcescu. It or any components may not be reproduced, republished, distributed, transmitted, displayed, broadcast or otherwise exploited in any manner without the express prior written permission of the author. The receipt or possession of this document does not convey any rights to reproduce, disclose, or distribute its contents, or to manufacture, use, or sell anything that it may describe, in whole or in part.

Introduction

Advertising is a fast-paced environment. Everything changes at the speed of light, consumers' options change quickly and, to benefit from it you need to stay on top of everything. I know it's challenging, I know it's difficult, but you need to do it because you can't grow your business if you don't pay attention to advertising. Consumers have become more demanding, and brands have become more important because everybody wants individuality. Each customer desires tailor-made products to satisfy not only their specific needs but also their specific values.

Do you know what the consumer seeks in our modern area? It's not the product. Nor the raw material. It is the personality. Yes, people nowadays (even yourself) when choosing a brand they are choosing it for its personality. Ten years ago you would choose a whitening toothpaste from a brand because it was the only brand who produced it. But now there are tens of brands producing it. So what makes you choose whitening toothpaste X from whitening toothpaste Y? Its personality. Like the movies, theatre plays and concerts, advertising is also offering a show. But it is a free-entrance show. The product is not for free; the entertainment is. So if you want to make the transition from spectators to consumers, you need to offer a hell of an entertainment. You need to give them reasons to choose you.

The "why" and the "how"

So, the world of advertising has changed, and content marketing is the newest tool. You shouldn't ask yourself why; you should ask yourself how. The "why" is easily explained. Consumers want to be engaged; they want to read and not only about your product. They want you to offer them ideas and advice. They don't get engaged anymore simply by finding out that your product exists. So what? There are billions of products on the market. They get excited if you provide them with qualitative information, so, in a manner of speaking, brands have become publishers.

Do you own a fragrance brand? Well, good news. You also own a TV station, a radio station, and a magazine. Why? Because commercials with pretty girls and boys, online banners or radio jingles just don't work anymore. Explanatory videos, articles about the history of fragrance or different ingredients, unique songs and other types of specialized content will do the trick.

The first rule is that you need to consider yourself a publisher also, no matter what type of industry you are in. The central idea behind content marketing is that if you provide your consumers with exciting, engaging and insightful information, they will buy from you because you are continually offering them reasons to believe that you know your business.

Let me offer you an example to show you how this works. Let's suppose there are two competitors, A and B. They both sell furniture. As a consumer wanting to redecorate my home, I will search on Google for "interior design ideas". Now, provider A has smart and optimized content on its blog, offering me interior design ideas, with pictures, trends, best materials, etc. My Google search will land me on A's blog, and after I read the article, I will become interested in A's products. The next step for me is that I will get to A's website, browse through different items and, eventually, if something catches my eye, I will buy. If I really like the products and the blog, and I consider the content to be valuable and engaging, I will subscribe to their blog. Thus, I will constantly receive news about their offers and, in no time, I will buy all my furniture from there. So, where is provider B in this picture? He doesn't exist. Why? Because my Google search doesn't consider him relevant; he doesn't offer me interior design ideas. And if Google doesn't consider him relevant, then he doesn't exist for me.

He may have better products and better prices than A, but, if I don't know about him, I can't buy from him, can I?

Take a moment to think about this. Then ask yourself which one of these two providers would you like to be? And so, through a mere imagination effort, the "why" is solved. Why? Because you need to exist in order to make sales. And existing nowadays in the world of advertising doesn't mean only awareness; it mostly means relevance.

The "how" is much more complicated, but, with the help of these steps, you will figure it out in no time. It's not rocket science; it's just advertising. There are situations when advertising is more complicated than rocket science. Fortunately, this is not one of them because there are a few simple steps you can follow to get your content marketing laboratory working perfectly.

Step 1: The Plan

Like any other type of marketing, content marketing also needs a plan. As **Zig Ziglar** used to say, *you were born to win; but, in order to be a winner you must plan to win, prepare to win and expect to win.* So, when planning your content marketing, the first question you need to ask yourself is what information you should communicate. Think about your consumer and their interests and needs. Put yourself in their shoes. Then, think about your brand, your unique selling proposition, and your expertise. Write down the answers for these two questions to get a clear image. Now think about the point where these two answers intersect, and that is your final answer. You should create content that answers your consumers' needs and also stresses your brand.

Think about your content as if it were a three-layer pyramid. The base of the pyramid gets your consumers'

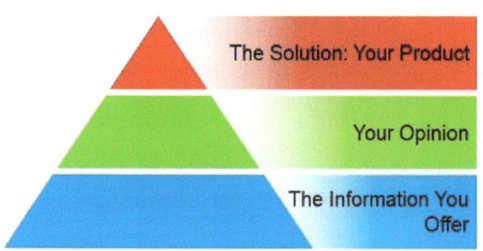

attention because it offers them valuable information they need. The middle of the pyramid gets them interested in you because your opinion on a particular matter proves to be credible and effective. The top of the pyramid shows them the solution they seek: your product. The outcome is that they are directed to your product.

Plan your content smartly. Each piece of content you provide your consumers with should have a clear objective. To view that specific objective, answer yourself some questions about your consumer. What are their issues and problems that need to be solved? What question do they need to answer? What kind of content can answer those questions? What kind of titles would let them know what you content is about? You should do this exercise for every piece of content you want to publish. It is the best way to make sure that you provide your consumers with relevant content to gain their trust and interest.

The next step is to decide how often you should produce content and what the best type of content for your business is. As you well know, content can be text, video or audio, so, according to the kind of business you run, you should decide on the type of content. Of course, you can combine different types, but you need to establish the main one. Afterward, you should decide on the tone of voice, how you want your consumers to perceive your brand.

Step 2: Who should produce the content?

Ok, you've established what kind of content you want to create. The next phase is to decide who will do this for you. To find the right people to produce your content is crucial to your success. You need to create a team from some of your internal people that specialize in marketing and advertising and, also, you will need the help of freelancers. Why is that?

Because your people know your business better; they've specialized in promoting your products or your services, they know the strategies, and they know your consumer's profile. On the other hand, freelancers specialize in content marketing, they know how to make the most of the content you publish, they are familiar with specific techniques and they know how to make the transition from consumer to audience. The best way to have excellent content is to mix the know-how of your people with the knowledge of freelancers in order to get the best results possible.

Also, you need a top managing editor in charge of the editorial calendar, of assigning content and monitoring the results. Think of the managing editor as the brain of a body. A body needs members and organs to function, and it  cannot operate without some of them, but the brain coordinates all the functions. Without a brain, you don't have a working body. The same is with your business. Without a very organized and analytical managing editor, your content will lack structure, and it will fail to accomplish its goals.

Step 3: What kind of content to produce?

This is one of the toughest decisions when it comes to content marketing because you really need to know your audience. The content you produce will mostly be about your consumer, not about you, at least not upfront. Of course, the objective of every piece of content is to direct the user towards your product, but you need to do that

subtly, firstly following their interests. If you fail to do so, the user will perceive your content as just another type of advertising, and it will lose its credibility, ultimately hurting your brand. So, the main question when it comes to content production is what are your consumers' interests? To answer this question, you need to do three things:

> **Talk to your employees.** From the sales teams to the secretary, each person in your organization has some insights about your brand. Some of them interact with your clients on a daily basis; some of them are just consumers of your brand. You shouldn't underestimate anyone, for each person can offer you valuable support. Ask them for ideas; engage them in conversations about what your clients need, etc. To motivate them, offer them incentives and rewards. Unlock their potential by

challenging them to come up with the best idea in a competition. You will be surprised how competitive people can be and how competitions tend to bring out the best in them.

- ➢ **Research your clients on social media.** Social media is the place where your clients voice their opinions clear and loudly, so look up their interests, their questions, what they ask on forums, what kind of blogs they read, etc. You can find out much stuff about your clients on social media, and this will help you develop tailor-made content just for them.

- ➢ **Conduct offline interviews with potential or actual clients.** Now, this method may be more expensive than the first two, but it will offer you great insights. You can either hire a research institute to come up with some answers, or you can do it yourself by using your sales team, sales reps or project-based employees. Go directly to your clients and ask them about their issues.

By combining these three methods, you will develop valuable insights that will help you design the main line of your content. It's easy. If you get to know what your clients need, then you also get to know how to get their attention. Furthermore, once you've gotten their attention, you can satisfy their needs and, in the end, offer your brand as a solution. That never fails.

After you've decided what your consumers' interests are, you also need to take into consideration other facts when planning your content strategy. Find out which are the trends in topics and try to relate your brand to them. Check out the search traffic and identify specific keywords to use in your content. If you do all these steps, you will have a strong content strategy that will stand out from your competition.

Step 4: How to produce and distribute your content?

This is one of the most challenging steps because, as a brand, you are not really used to also being a publisher. A piece of content often requires the work of an idea generator, a content creator, a graphic designer, a managing editor and an SEO expert. In addition, in the whole process, there are also involved the people who work in social media, the people from the legal and PR departments and the marketing executives. With so many people participating in this process, it can become challenging to produce content as if you were a publisher.

But, with the right type of organizing, this process can become very smooth. Firstly, you need to have an editorial calendar in which to plan all the content you will publish. All the people involved in the process should have access to this calendar in order to plan their actions. Make sure the calendar is always up to date and that the information it provides is very clear.

When it comes to distributing your content, keep in mind that your blog should be your primary channel. You need to have consistency in your blog. Also, to engage people, all the information should be in one place, so that if your consumer is interested in an article, they will also get the chance to read similar articles. And, who knows, maybe, if your content is very attractive, you will get many visitors on your blog, and you will be able to also use it as a cross-marketing tool.

While your blog should be your main channel, don't forget about other channels that offer you visibility. Post all your content on your blog, but don't resume to this channel only. Use social media like Facebook, Twitter, LinkedIn, Tumblr, Google+ and other channels that will ensure you the awareness you need for your content. Also, if you have video content, eBooks or infographics, don't forget about YouTube, SlideShare, and Pinterest. By using the proper mix of channels of distribution, you will make sure your content reaches the audience and gets you the results you need for your business to thrive.

Step 5: How to get an audience for your content?

Now you know how to plan your content strategy, how to develop your team, how to create your content and how to distribute it. But how do you get an audience for it? Which are the best ways to build an audience for your content?

To build your audience, you need to find out who are the ones that can help you. Firstly, there are the organizations or the persons who get a lot of traffic on their websites. It's quite logical. They have a great distribution channel, and you have content that needs to reach an audience. But don't just select them based only on traffic. For example, if you are selling software products, it is probably not a good idea to advertise your content through a culinary blog, no matter how many visitors they get.

You need to have consistency in the communication and, thus, you need to select the organizations or individuals that have the best traffic, but in your area of expertise. So how can you get in touch with them? Don't just contact them and ask them to do things for you. Share their articles and postings; follow their activity; place comments on their blogs. Once you become visible for them, ask for their help with your content. Provide them with compelling content that suits their interests and ask them to help you out, with mutual benefits. Make barter in terms of distributing the content; help them out with what they publish and get their help for what you publish.

Next you have to think about the search engines. If your content is relevant to your consumer, the search engines will help your rank, driving traffic to your website. But how do you make your content relevant to the user? This is more of a research phase that you need to do. Having your clients in mind, conduct a research to find out what are keywords they type when searching for certain information. After you've identified those keywords, make sure that every piece of content you publish is optimized for them.

Next, in order to see if you are doing it right, monitor the way those optimized keywords affect your ranking and your traffic. This phase needs a lot of patience, but it is worth it. If you're asking yourself how exactly it is worth it, then think like a consumer. Whenever you are searching for something on Google, how many times do you get past the first page?

Optimizing your content and getting individuals and organizations to distribute it for you is required, but you should also take into consideration advertising your content through paid tactics. Use the sponsored ads on Facebook, the paid email distribution, etc.

At this point, you are probably wondering why you should have an advertising budget for your content, which is also a type of advertising, instead of using that money to advertise your products directly. The thing is that people are used to ads about products. They have developed a system to ignore them as if they didn't really exist. Using money to pay for Facebook ads for your products isn't as efficient as using the money to advertise your content. For every 10 people that see your ads on your product on Facebook, 2 of them will actually click on it to see what it is about. That means you get 2 people for every ad you place. Now, if your ad is about interesting and relevant content for them, there's a pretty good chance that out of 10 people, 5 will click it. And, as you are using the exact amount of money for both of the ads, you can see for yourself which is more relevant: 2 people or 5 people.

Step 6: How to transform your readers into clients?

I know you've been waiting for this step from the beginning, but you have to put everything in order before you start thinking about this. Now that your content is being properly published and distributed, you have a lot of readers and a big audience. That's great, but how do you turn your readers into buyers?

The ideal visitor will see your content, notice your product and contact your sales team to ask for more details or to buy it. But this is not the case for every visitor you get, so you need to start thinking about the others, for they represent the majority of your audience.

The first rule to make this transition is to convince them to come back for more. In order for that to happen, your content needs to always be sharp and relevant to your consumers so that somebody who visits your website for the first time, finds himself or herself in the situation where they want to see more. Make sure that the subscription option is visible to your visitors, but don't bug them with banners over the content and stuff like that. They will reject your content and never visit your website again. Make your subscription button visible and clear, but not intrusive.

The next step is to always optimize your content for this transition. What I mean is that while short videos and articles are available to all the users, make sure that you also produce content like eBooks or longer videos that require your visitors to leave their contact information in order to access them. This way, you will get a valuable database which you can use to send offers and newsletters to your visitors, making them interested in your product or service.

So, how to make the final sale? Well, you've got all the tools now. You've got a valuable database and, moreover, you've got details about your consumers from what they read. So, make it personal. Approach them on a personal way because you already know what they want. You're not walking in the dark anymore; you have turned on a light that lets you see your potential buyers. Seeing them means knowing what they want and that leads to making the final sale. Design your marketing campaigns according to their profile. You know their needs; empathize with them. Make them acknowledge their needs by showing them that you get them. Then offer the solution to their needs: your product/service.

Step 7: Monitor your content and the results it brings you.

While this is the final step in creating a valuable and efficient content marketing laboratory, is it also the most important because, even if you are doing everything by the book, you may not get it right at first. The market is unpredictable, so you need to stay ahead of things and be proactive. And you do that by always monitoring the relation between what you publish and the results you get.

How to do a correct and efficient monitoring? You just need to ask yourself a couple of questions. Firstly, you should ask yourself if you have enough ideas for your content. Think of the main things you want people to know about your product/service. Then, count the unique ideas in your content. See if those two fit together. Then, after analyzing your content, discover which piece of content had the best ideas/results and identify who created it. Thus, you will identify your best content creator and make sure your team is always efficient.

Ask yourself if the content you produce follows your editorial calendar without any delays. This is important because you need to be as productive as you can. Next, think about your distribution. Ask yourself whether your channels of distribution are enough to reach all of your potential buyers or clients and, afterwards, identify the channels that bring you the most visitors. Try to optimize the channels that don't perform very well and invest more in those who do a great job. Then, identify the blogs and the organizations that bring you the most traffic. You've got a limited amount of space for bartering the content you produce, so make sure you use it wisely.

Also, check up on how well your paid ads are performing. Consider the link between how much you invest in them and how many results you get. Consider your new visitors and ask yourself what kind of content attracts them. Consider your older visitor and see which type of content keeps them engaged. Next, think about your audience and try to find out whether each of them is satisfied with what they receive. In the end, after you've answered all these questions, see if you need to revisit some of your tactics. Remember that change is not a bad thing; it just means you're on the path to success.

Golden rules of content marketing

You've been through all the steps now, but you still need to know certain facts about content marketing. Like any other type of marketing, content marketing also has its rules. Here are the golden rules of content marketing which, if you follow, will lead to your success in this new type of marketing.

1. **Question asked – question answered**. When one of your visitors or clients asks you a question, answer it promptly. Don't delay the answer, don't be vague.

2. **Helpful and smart – not intelligent and arrogant.** Be friendly towards your consumers. Your content doesn't need to prove how intelligent you are and how little they know. It just needs to prove you have the right expertise and you are willing to help them.

3. **Listen more, speak less**. I know you are publishing content and this may seem contradictory but, if you listen to your consumers and to the people around you, you will get valuable insights. Thus, your content will always be relevant and you will always have great ideas.

4. **The old "call to action".** You don't want to bug your visitors with tons of advertising messages but you also don't want to publish simple information. After all, you are not a newspaper. Find the balance between relevant information and call to action.

5. **Stay unbiased**. You need to earn their trust, so don't communicate in a biased way.

6. **Tell them a good story.** Deep down inside, we are all children searching for a really great story. We remember stories and we tend to forget facts. It doesn't mean that you should actually publish stories. But dress up your facts into interesting stories.

7. **Be a teacher.** People search for information because they want to learn. Be their teacher. But don't act arrogant; teach them what you know and they will reward you with their trust.

8. **Stay passionate and enthusiastic.** We are all attracted to people who are passionate because they have the talent to unlock our inner passion. We get more interested in people who are genuinely enthusiastic about what they do because it means they are really doing something good.

9. **Be a leader.** From the ancient times, people have always needed somebody to look up to. Every industry needs a leader, someone who possesses the best expertise. Attract your consumers by showing them your leadership.

10. **Be careful about the quality of your content.** Every piece of content you publish needs to be more than

ok; it needs to be wow. If it's just average content, then it will also affect the pieces of content you publish that are really great.

11. **Don't try to be perfect;** try, instead to be your best possible self every day. Perfect doesn't mean evolution for perfect is frozen and static. Better means evolving; show your consumers that you can become better every day and they will ask for more.

12. **Consider your client, not the competition.** So what if your competitor publishes content on a certain subject? It doesn't mean that you should do it too. Nor does it mean you shouldn't do it. The point is that, when it comes to content marketing, the only factor that is relevant in dictating what kind of content you should publish is your client; not the competition.

13. **Don't forget that everybody has a story.** While most of the people don't realize their own story, it's your job to bring it to the surface for them by using your content.

14. **Your industry has a story.** Yes, each industry has its own story. Whether is the secret ingredient Cleopatra used in her fragrance or the symbol of bracelets worn by

warriors, you've got a story. Publish it and get people's attention.

15. **Don't think about content marketing as a program you need to implement**; instead, think about it a cultural movement and people will follow you.

16. **Make your opinion known to the world.** You are a leader, act like one. Take a strong opinion and let people know what you are thinking.

17. **Don't communicate only who you are**; communicate also who you are not. You need to make a difference. People are tired of hearing what things are. They get more interested when hearing what things aren't.

18. **Don't let the legal department inflict themselves too much upon your content.** Yes, you need their expertise and advice, but don't let them dictate the kind of content you publish. They are not marketers.

19. **Remember that consumers think in manners of their problems.** They don't think, at first, what you can offer them; they think about what they need. Create your content with this in mind and only in the end offer your

product/service as a solution. Don't publish about you; publish about them.

20. **Don't let the fact that other marketers have addressed the same issue as the one you are planning to address to stop you.** Is not about the issue itself; it is about your opinion on it.

21. **Engage them, but don't forget to be useful.** Great content is both engaging and useful. Don't harm the usefulness of your content for its amazingness.

22. **Simple answers don't always make for great answers.** Yes, you need to have clear answers but you also need to take into consideration that not everybody acts and thinks the same. Thus, your answers should always be calibrated to your audience and you should always state that it may not apply for some people.

23. **Be your own customer.** While creating content, don't think as a marketer first. Think as a consumer and try to think about what would engage you and what you would want to see.

24. **Remember that content marketing is a tool**, not the final outcome. You will travel through this whole

process of content marketing, but while you do, always keep in mind your goal. Even if you don't publish content about your product, keep in mind that its role is to increase your sales.

25. **Don't try too hard to let people know you are the expert.** If you try too hard, they will perceive you as a fake. Trust them to find out for themselves about your expertise. Stay focused and publish great content and, in the end, they will perceive you as an expert.

26. **People want different things**. Why should you choose only a type of audience when you can have more? Some of your visitors will want to read, some of them just want to listen and some of them want to watch videos. Use a mix of communication to ensure that you are relevant to more types of audience.

28. **Content marketing is here to stay**. Don't forget about this and don't dismiss it as just a trend. Give it your best shot and watch the results.

A few words in the end

Don't forget that these steps and rules are explanatory for how to get started with content marketing. You can learn the basics and you should. But to continue with content marketing you should always be ahead of things.

Regard it as an efficient tool for your brand. If you come to think about it, content marketing is more affordable than other types of advertising and more personal. It's like your personal stamp, the voice of your brand. Think about all the greatness it can bring you. For never in the history of advertising have brands been so personal.

While other types of advertising speak about your brand, content marketing speaks about your consumer and shows that you really pay attention to them. As a result, content marketing is an opportunity for you to distinguish yourself and to build your brand in a unique original way.

We are unique human beings, thus we seek unique things. Nourish your content marketing and see your business thrive.

www.ingramcontent.com/pod-product-compliance
Lightning Source LLC
Chambersburg PA
CBHW041611180526
45159CB00002BC/812